IMAGES
of America

FERRIES OF
SAN FRANCISCO BAY

1. Aden Brothers
2. Alameda Ferry
3. Angel Island-Tiburon Ferry
4. Atcheson, Topeka & Santa Fe Ry.
5. Blue & Gold Fleet
6. California Northwestern R.R.
7. California Pacific R.R.
8. Central Pacific R.R.
9. Contra Costa Steam Navigation Co.
10. Golden Gate Bridge, Highway & Transportation District
11. Golden Gate Ferry
12. Harbor Bay Ferry
13. Key System
14. Mare Island Ferry
15. Martinez-Benicia Ferry
16. Monticello Steamship Co.

A. Alcatraz Is.
B. Angel Is.
C. Ferry Bldg.
D. Hyde St. Pier
E. Mare Is.
F. Meiggs Wharf
G. Oakland S.P. Mole
H. Pier 41
I. S.P. Shipyard
J. W.P. Mole
K. Yerba Buena Is.

17. Nickel Ferry
18. North Pacific Coast R.R.
19. North Shore R.R.
20. Northwestern Pacific R.R.
21. Richmond-San Rafael Ferry
22. Rodeo-Vallejo Ferry
23. Sacramento Northern Ry.
24. San Francisco & Alameda R.R.
25. San Francisco & North Pacific R.R.
26. Saucelito Land & Ferry Co.
27. Six Minute Ferry
28. South Pacific Coast R.R.
29. Southern Pacific-Golden Gate Ferries, Ltd.
30. Southern Pacific R.R.
31. Vallejo BayLink
32. Western Pacific R.R.

Not drawn to scale

SUISUN BAY

MALLARD

NAPA RIVER

SO. VALLEJO
VALLEJO

SOLANO CO.

MORROW COVE

BENICIA

MARTINEZ

PORT COSTA

CROCKETT
VALLEJO JCT.
RODEO

CONTRA COSTA CO.

DONAHUE LANDING

SONOMA CO.

PETALUMA CREEK

SAN PABLO BAY

RICHMOND

BERKELEY

ALAMEDA CO.

OAKLAND

ALAMEDA

POINT SAN QUENTIN

LARKSPUR LANDING

TIBURON

MARIN CO.

SAN FRANCISCO BAY

SAUSALITO

SAN FRANCISCO

PACIFIC OCEAN

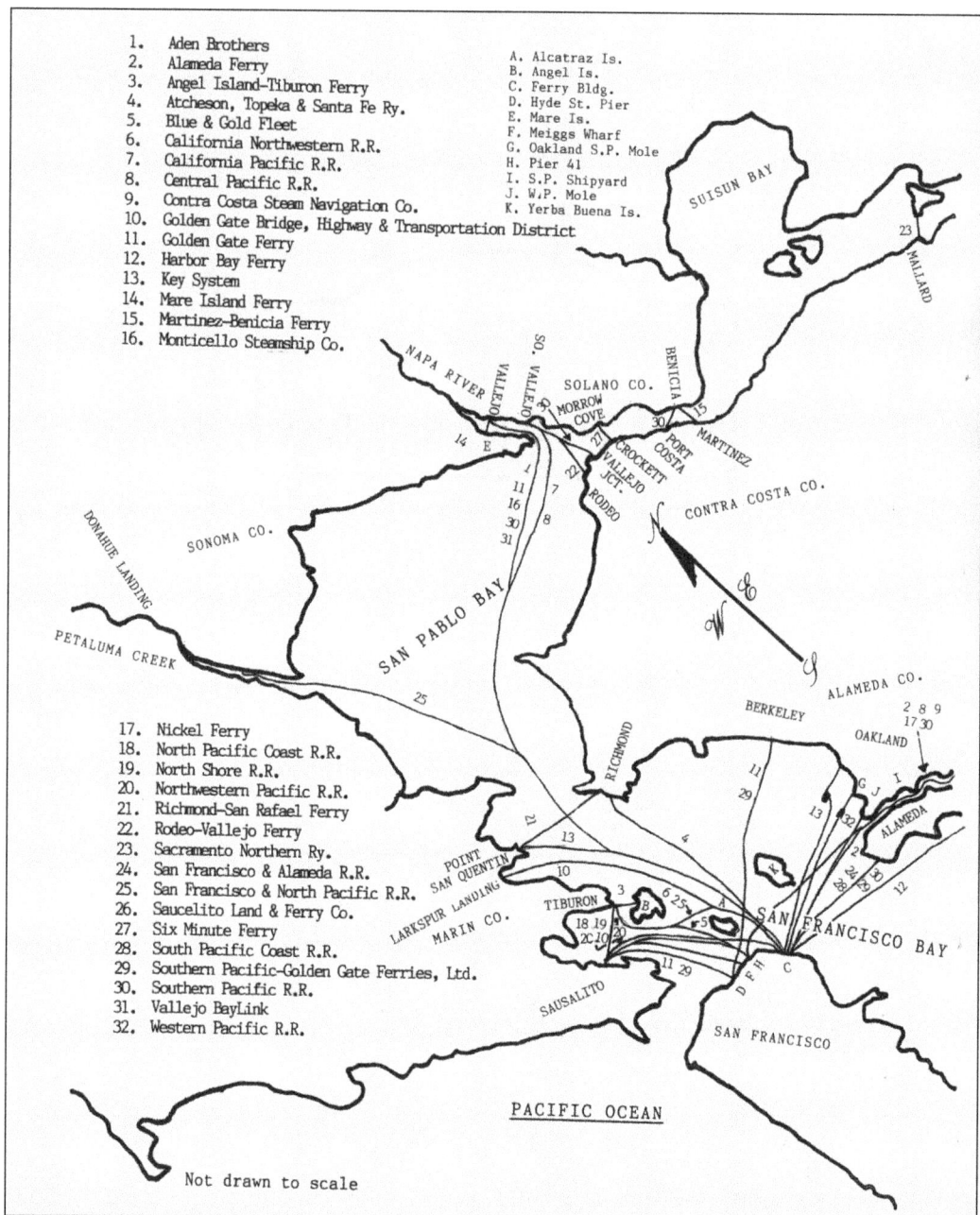

This sketch map shows, in general, the routes of the ferry operators covered in this book as well as the extent of the San Francisco Bay ferryboat travel. (Drawn by the author.)

ON THE COVER: The twin-stacker *Santa Clara*, with paddle wheels in reverse to slow the ferry and her sponsons clearly showing, drifts into her slip at the Ferry Building in 1929. The deckhand at center is ready to pull out the pin, which has locked the forward rudder as part of changing ends for the return trip to the Southern Pacific's Oakland Mole. (Southern Pacific photograph; Bill Knorp collection.)

IMAGES
of America

FERRIES OF
SAN FRANCISCO BAY

Paul C. Trimble
with William Knorp

ARCADIA
PUBLISHING

Published by Arcadia Publishing
Charleston, South Carolina

Library of Congress Catalog Card Number: 2006938686

For all general information contact Arcadia Publishing at:
Telephone 843-853-2070
Fax 843-853-0044
E-mail sales@arcadiapublishing.com
For customer service and orders:
Toll-Free 1-888-313-2665

Visit us on the Internet at www.arcadiapublishing.com

To my brother Tom, who rode the ferries with me;
to my sister-in-law Gail, who somehow puts up with me; and
to the memory of John C. Alioto, Jr., my friend and collaborator,
who had wanted to do this book with me.

CONTENTS

ACKNOWLEDGMENTS

This book could never have been written without ferryboat historian William Knorp. Bill encouraged the project and was always ready to help, either with his bottomless repository of information or his photograph collection.

Thanks are due to those many historians and photographers, known and unknown, who preserved ferryboat history for future generations. Without them the rich history of San Francisco Bay ferries would long ago have been lost.

Special thanks go to fellow Arcadia authors and historians Emiliano Echevarria; Jim Kern, director of the Vallejo Naval and Historical Museum; and John V. Robinson. Thanks also goes to Gus Campagna, secretary of the Northwestern Pacific Railroad Historical Society and custodian of the NWPRRHS Archives; Bill Kooiman of the J. Porter Shaw Library, San Francisco National Maritime Museum National Historical Park; and Betty Maffi of the Contra Costa Historical Society. All aided me many times in my quest for pictures and information. Thanks are also due to the Blue and Gold Fleet, John Reduik and Capt. Maggie McDonogh of the Angel Island–Tiburon ferry, and Mary Curry of the Golden Gate Bridge, Highway and Transportation District for their assistance.

Thanks go to the staff at Arcadia publishing for their patience and understanding during critical times as this book was in preparation.

Special thanks again to my daughter Debbie for acting as an unofficial editor, doing the computer work, and being the fourth generation Trimble in America to have worked in printing and publishing. I am proud.

Lastly, we must note those many ferryboat builders, skippers, and crews, as well as their passengers, who made this history in the first place.

INTRODUCTION

A half-century has passed since the last major automobile ferries and the last conventional passenger ferries crossed San Francisco Bay. Yet memories of them linger, taking us back to when America had only 48 states and when there were no touch-tone telephones, color televisions, computers, digital watches, calculators, DVD players, cell phones, or other gadgets, which today are as much taken for granted as the ferryboats were in their day.

In recent years, there has been a revival of ferry travel on the San Francisco Bay, yet with suburban sprawl miles away from shore and without effective feeder systems, they are less than a totally efficient mode of transport for today's commuters. By contrast, most of the old ferries were linked with railways and a higher density of living and working areas, making them models which today's planners would do well to emulate, for overall, they were indispensable to the economy and well-being of the San Francisco Bay Area.

With stacks belching black smoke, steam whistles sounding signals to other maritime craft, and bells clanging from atop the pilothouses or hurricane decks, the ferries carried millions upon millions of passengers who were afforded such amenities as restaurants, saloons, candy and cigar stands, glorious views of the world's largest landlocked harbor (or the fog, as the case may be), and a chance to read the newspapers. Commuters formed social groups with regular seats, and woe unto any interloper who chanced to occupy the seat of a "regular!"

Fifty-six years ago, the author was privileged, along with his Cub Scout pack, to visit the pilothouse of an Oakland-San Francisco steamer, perhaps the *Berkeley* or the *Sacramento*. The gracious captain showed us his domain, explaining this and that, and then called for questions. The first came from the author, who pointed to the deck next to the wheel where there was a white enamel bowl half filled with an amber liquid of an obnoxious nature and asked, "What's that?" The only response was adult laughter.

Alas, the cuspidors are gone, along with the steamers themselves, their legacies sustained by old movies, books, models, photographs, memorabilia, and occasionally a preserved craft. Soon there will be no one left with the personal memories, and these items will have to suffice.

This book's purpose is to preserve those memories, whether of the ferryboat fan, the former commuter, the traveler, or the young boy who wanted to grow up to become a ferryboat captain, and to extend them to the generations who will never experience the thrills we had while crossing the bay's waters on a steam-powered, double-ended sidewheeler.

It was June 1955 in this photograph, when people still dressed for train travel. The author, then 15, rode the ferryboat *Eureka* from San Francisco to the Oakland Mole to catch the Southern Pacific (SP) candy train *City of San Francisco*, bound for Chicago. To his left were his brother Tom, age 8, and his best friend Perry Weddle, almost 16. (Trimble collection.)

One

EAST BAY TO SAN FRANCISCO

The ferryboats from San Francisco to the East Bay remain foremost in the minds of those for whom nostalgia is paramount. Those routes were long dominated by the white ferries of the Southern Pacific Railroad, which used them to transfer railroad passengers, commuters, and automobiles. Indeed, the SP, or "Espee," fleet—at one time the world's largest—essentially closed the book on the ferryboat era when the *San Leandro* made her final revenue voyage in 1958.

The Espee wasn't the only ferry operator between San Francisco and Alameda and Contra Costa Counties. The Atcheson, Topeka, and Santa Fe Railway ran ferries between Richmond and the city for the benefit of its rail passengers, as did the Western Pacific Railroad, operating from Oakland.

The Key Route, an Alameda County transit conglomerate, operated a fleet of orange boats between San Francisco and Oakland to connect with the Key Route's interurban trains. Another interurban, the Sacramento Northern Railway, also used the Key Route ferries.

As automobiles increased in number, the SP built auto ferries to accommodate them, thus promoting the very vehicles that would one day put the wonderful old ferries out of business.

Meiggs Wharf in San Francisco reached 2,000 feet north from what is now Powell and Francisco Streets. Meiggs Wharf hosted square-riggers as well as early-day ferryboats from Marin County. Today it is filled in and the site of Fisherman's Wharf, five blocks east of the Hyde Street Pier. (Emiliano Echevarria collection.)

In the early 1880s, ferryboat arrivals and departures at the Central Pacific Railroad ferry shed in San Francisco were already creating traffic from cable cars, horsecars, coaches, hansoms, broughams, and hacks, not to mention pedestrians, as this print from a cracked glass-plate negative shows. (Trimble collection.)

During the 1920s and 1930s, San Francisco's Ferry Building was the terminus for ferryboats connecting four steam railroads and five interurban systems with 29 city streetcar and cable car lines, resulting in over 55 million passengers per year, a figure exceeded only by London's Charing Cross Station. (Trimble collection.)

San Francisco's Ferry Building was humming with business during the 1920s, as (pictured from left to right) the SP auto ferries *New Orleans* and *El Paso*; the Western Pacific's *Feather River*; and the SP's *Encinal*, destined for Oakland via the "Creek Route," await departure time. (Bill Knorp collection.)

Bert Ward made one of the author's favorite photographs, capturing the *Thoroughfare II* arriving at the Ferry Building from Oakland, the WP ferry *Feather River*, the *Berkeley*, and the twin-stacker *Alameda*. Passengers boarded from the Y-shaped ramps to the cabin decks and off-loaded from the maindecks. (The late Bert H. Ward photograph; Trimble collection.)

In 1939, the East Bay interurbans began running over the Bay Bridge into a new terminal at First and Mission Streets in San Francisco. The city streetcars were rerouted accordingly, but more people drove instead of riding the trains, and the substantial loss of streetcar ridership changed forever the city's transportation pattern. (Trimble collection.)

The Bay Bridge opened to motor vehicles in 1937, two years before the trains utilized the bridge. A decade later, the once voluminous ferry fleet was down to four boats, decimating streetcar ridership from the Ferry Building. Here a nearly empty streetcar departs in 1947. (Trimble collection.)

By 1950, reduced ferry ridership had irreparably damaged San Francisco's public-transit system. Moreover, minus the pedestrians from the ferries, the foot of Market Street went into economic decay. Buses replacing the streetcars went to the landmark only because they had no other place to turn around. (Trimble collection.)

From the *San Leandro*'s deck, the Oakland Mole is visible. At center is where passengers off-loaded from the maindeck, and at center right is the raised apron and boarding gangway. The mole's days are ending and the slip, victim of countless beatings from ferries hulls, shows it. (NWPRRHS Archives, Hogarty collection.)

By 1940, the Oakland Mole was a quieter place as the SP's interurbans began running directly into San Francisco in 1939, and the ferry fleet, once the world's largest, was down to only four boats. The mole continued to host passenger trains of the Western Pacific, Santa Fe, and SP until 1960, when a 50-year lease expired and the property reverted to the Port of Oakland. (Ken Kidder photograph; Trimble collection.)

Transfers from one vehicle or mode to another is always a problem in public transportation. To minimize the inconvenience, the Southern Pacific Oakland Mole brought the ferries and trains into closer proximity than will be found in some contemporary ferry facilities. (Trimble collection.)

Southern Pacific trains, both steam and electric, met the SP ferries at the Oakland Mole at the foot of Seventh Street. At left is a Sacramento-bound local, while at the right, the *Overland Limited*, in two sections, has arrived from Chicago. This was in 1934 when steam was king on the Espee. (The late Ralph W. Demoro photograph; Trimble collection.)

16

Alameda's passengers rode the Southern Pacific's electric Red Trains directly to the ferry terminal, an arrangement common to most of the Bay Area's major ferry terminals. To the left of the terminal building is the driveway to the SP automobile ferries from Alameda to San Francisco. (Trimble collection.)

The Southern Pacific ferryboats had to meet railroad timetables, which were run with military precision. The Alameda Mole also contained the slip for SP auto ferries. By advertising auto ferries as "cheapest way to cross the bay," one has to wonder if SP was surrendering to the inevitable. (Trimble collection.)

The Contra Costa Steam Navigation Company's *Contra Costa* (right) and the California Pacific Railroad's *Capital* are at San Francisco's Davis Street wharf around 1869. The former, built in 1857, offered ferry services to Oakland and later to Point San Quentin, while the latter connected with trains at South Vallejo. (NWPRRHS Archives, Stindt collection.)

The *Oakland* was rebuilt by the SP in 1875 from the riverboat *Chrysopolis*, built in 1860. On January 27, 1940, just after her retirement and sale to junkers, the *Oakland* caught fire and burned to her waterline, still bearing her original engine. (Bill Knorp collection.)

The cabin-deck interior of the *Oakland* meant style, and the Southern Pacific did its best to keep everything shipshape, from gleaming white paint to varnished woods and polished brasses. The reader should note the absence of vandalism of any kind. (NWPRRHS Archives; Hogarty collection.)

Below maindecks, in the engine room of the *Oakland*, the engineer (in SP uniform) mans the controls on direct orders from the pilothouse. The *Oakland*'s original 1860 engine remained when the ferry was rebuilt from the *Chrysopolis* in 1875, lasting until retirement in 1940. (Bill Knorp collection.)

The *Oakland* never had a serious accident. Considering the millions of crossings on San Francisco Bay, the ferries were incredibly safe. Of the dozen serious accidents, in only five were any lives lost. The known deaths from ferry accidents totals only 71, and none since the year 1928. (Bill Knorp collection.)

20

The *Amador*, seen departing the Ferry Building around 1900, was built in 1869 for the Central Pacific as a single ender for both riverboating and ferrying, as her maindeck contour reveals. In 1878, she became a double-ender. The captain in the wheelhouse is holding the wheel with his left hand while his right is on the telegraph, signaling orders to the engineer. The *Amador* was retired in 1904 and served as a clubhouse for the University of California rowing crews. In 1915, she was blown up in a fireboat demonstration at the Panama-Pacific International Exposition in San Francisco. (Bill Knorp collection.)

The *El Capitan* was the first vessel built in the CPRR yards in Oakland, serving until November 1925—an endurance of 57 years. Her maiden voyage on June 21, 1868, was an excursion under Capt. Edward Hackett for politicians, lawyers, bankers, businessmen, and spouses. All were treated to a huge breakfast and a string ensemble. On February 19, 1879, she was rammed by the *Alameda* and partially sunk but was refloated that same year to serve again. (San Francisco National Maritime Museum, Trimble collection.)

The *Alameda I*, built in 1866 as the first double-decked double-ender on San Francisco Bay, was successively operated by the San Francisco and Alameda, Central Pacific, and the Southern Pacific Railroads until broken up in 1898. Most Bay Area ferries were railroad owned at one time or another. (Trimble collection.)

Built in 1883, the *Piedmont* served both the CPRR and the SP and was the first ferryboat into the new Ferry Building on a revenue run. For many years a mainstay on the Alameda–San Francisco route, she was retired in 1940 and dismantled later that year. (Bill Knorp collection.)

Not all ferries had walking beams. The *Piedmont* had a single-cylinder horizontal engine, with the energy going directly to the crankshaft driving the sidewheels. Her 14-foot piston stroke was the longest of any marine engine in the world. Water from the San Francisco Bay was used for steam. (NWPRRHS Archives; Hogarty collection.)

Even below the maindecks, in the engine rooms, such as on the *Piedmont*, where steam, grease, grime, and sweat held forth, the ferryboats' brass was kept polished and shipshape. The crews' pride in their vessels helped give the ferries a dignity that was never relinquished. (NWPRRHS Archives; Hogarty collection.)

The cabin deck of the *Piedmont* reflected craftmanship not seen today, except in museums. In 1888, the *Piedmont* became the first SP ferry to be equipped with incandescent lights. Indeed, when the *Piedmont*'s transbay crossings ended, the SP was reluctant to dispose of her until 1944. (The late Robert Parkinson photograph; NWPRRHS Archives; Hogarty collection.)

Built in 1898, the screw steamer *Berkeley* was, at the time, the fastest ferry on the bay, and she ruined many a piling when pulling into her slips due to her speed. In this view, the *Berkeley* leaves San Francisco as the *San Rafael* approaches from Sausalito. (Bill Knorp collection.)

The *Berkeley* was nothing if not durable, having spent 60 years on the Espee lists. Shown here in 1898 arriving in San Francisco from Oakland, the *Berkeley* was sold in 1959 to be moored as a floating emporium in Sausalito, followed by a new career in 1973 as a maritime museum in San Diego. In the background is the *San Rafael* arriving from Sausalito. (Trimble collection.)

The *Garden City*, built in 1879 for the South Pacific Coast, steams past the Western Pacific Mole about 1920 and up the San Antonio Creek, now the Oakland Estuary, to port at the foot of Broadway. Retired in 1929, she became a fishing resort on the Carquinez Strait, just east of Crockett. (Trimble collection.)

The *Garden City* steams out of the Oakland Estuary's "Creek Route" on its way to the Ferry Building in this 1919 image. The background shows the Western Pacific Railroad's mole and trains. The estuary was not a safe route until dredging of the sandbars beneath the shoal waters, after which it was popular for taking people to what was once the center of Oakland. (John V. Robinson collection.)

The SP retired the *Garden City* after 50 years of service in June 1929. She was taken to the Carquinez Strait to be used as a fishing resort and, in 1936, was again purchased and towed to a pier at Eckley, near Crockett, to become a dance hall, dining room, and bar. In the 1950s, she was abandoned altogether and left to rot. (John V. Robinson photograph.)

In 1983, a disastrous fire swept the hills between Crockett and Port Costa, destroying a lot of local history. Included in the conflagration were what was left of Eckley and the ferry *Garden City*, leaving only a charred mess. (John V. Robinson photograph.)

The *Alameda II*, at 1,320 tons and with a 273-foot steel hull, was built in 1913 by the Espee, which ran her until 1945 when she was burned for scrap. This double-ended sidewheeler with two three-cylinder compound engines was a sister ship to the *Santa Clara*. (Trimble collection.)

The *Santa Clara* (pictured here) and the *Alameda II* were sister ships and the only twin stackers in the SP fleet. Built in 1915, the *Santa Clara* was powered by a brace of compound engines. This handsome vessel was burned for scrap in 1945. (The late Wilbur C. Whittaker photograph; Trimble collection.)

When built in 1877, the *Newark* sported two 42-foot paddle wheels, the largest of any sidewheeler anywhere. They were later replaced by 29-foot paddle wheels. SP ferries on the "Creek Route" had competition from the Nickel Ferry between 1893 and 1895, which used the *Rosalie* and *Alvira*. Named for its single-trip fare, the Nickel Ferry's only legacy was to have the formerly competitive tariff in place well into the 1930s. (San Francisco Maritime NHP.)

The SP shipyard at the foot of Oakland's Peralta Street dated back to 1868 and the building of the ferry *El Capitan*. The shipyard built, rebuilt, and repaired SP's navy of ferries and riverboats. Here the *Newark* is being rebuilt into the *Sacramento*. (Trimble collection.)

Fresh from being rebuilt from the old *Newark* at the SP shipyard, the new *Sacramento* is pictured on her "sea trials" on San Francisco Bay. This accounts for her paddle wheels being still and the lack of smoke from her stack. (Bill Knorp collection.)

Generations of children and adults stood fascinated at the glassed-in fiddley (see glossary) of a ferry, in this case the *Sacramento*, watching the giant steam piston driving the walking beam, which powered the crankshaft propelling the paddle wheels in what seemed to be an endless up-and-down rhythm. (Bill Knorp collection.)

Among the San Francisco Bay ferryboat aficionados is Bill Knorp, who has ridden them, photographed them, and collected information about them. In the 1940s, Knorp was photographed while forward of the *Sacramento's* wheelhouse, which was usually off limits to passengers. (Bill Knorp collection.)

Rebuilt from the old *Newark* in 1923, the *Sacramento* was the SP's last passenger ferry. She remained in service on the Oakland run until 1956, when she was sold and sent to Redondo Beach, California, to become a fishing barge. This 1939 picture shows the *Sacramento* leaving Oakland. (Bill Knorp collection.)

The *Transit*, launched in 1876, was the CPRR's second ferryboat used for moving freight cars across San Francisco Bay. The *Transit* was retired by the SP in February 1934 after 58 years of service. This photograph was taken around 1931. (Bill Knorp collection.)

The *Encinal* was built in 1888 for the South Pacific Coast Railroad, connecting Alameda with San Francisco. While the *Encinal* was still on her ways, the SPC was bought by Southern Pacific, and the grand old ferry made her career on Oakland's "Creek Route." (Bill Knorp collection.)

In 1908, the 2,662-ton *Melrose* was the first of the San Francisco Bay's ferries built specifically for automobiles. In this 1919 scene, the *Melrose* is arriving at the Ferry Building from the "Creek Route." In 1929, she went to Southern Pacific–Golden Gate Ferries, but in 1931 was retired and dismantled. (Bill Knorp collection.)

Californians embraced the automobile as soon as they could afford them, and the Southern Pacific responded by building the *Thoroughfare II* in 1912 to ferry cars across the bay. The second *Thoroughfare* was retired from service in 1935. (Bill Knorp collection.)

In 1922, the SP built three additional auto ferries: the *San Mateo* (above), *Shasta*, and *Yosemite*. The SP auto ferries kept tradition with ladies' restrooms on the cabin decks and those for men on the maindecks. Espee ferryboats and locomotives burned crude oil for fuel, and it showed. (Trimble collection.)

The *New Orleans*, built in 1924, was a sister ship to the *El Paso* and the *Klamath*. All three went to the Richmond–San Rafael ferry after the Bay Bridge effectively ended automobile ferries between the East Bay and San Francisco. (Trimble collection.)

The *Klamath* was added to the SP fleet in 1925, a decade when automobile growth in San Francisco and Alameda County soared by 201,959. The auto ferries had jukeboxes, and people could listen to music while crossing the bay. In 1964, the *Klamath* became a floating office building in San Francisco. (Trimble collection.)

In 1927, the Southern Pacific built three new diesel-electric ferries: *Lake Tahoe*, *Stockton*, and *Fresno*, pictured heading for the Ferry Building in her Southern Pacific–Golden Gate Ferries livery. In 1938, she went to Puget Sound to become the *Willapa*. (Bill Knorp collection.)

The *Lake Tahoe*, pictured here, and sister ships *Fresno* and *Stockton* were the SP's first use of diesel-electric engines, predating SP diesel locomotives. The *Lake Tahoe*, under Capt. Edward Hallin, made the last auto-ferry crossing between San Francisco and the East Bay on May 16, 1940, arriving in Oakland at 9:40 p.m. (James Carpenter photograph; Bill Knorp collection.)

For two decades, San Francisco's Hyde Street Pier hosted Golden Gate Ferry and SP auto ferries. Before World War II, this area was largely industrial, attracting foot passengers, as it was a direct commute to nearby jobs. Today this area is part of the National Maritime Museum. (Emiliano Echevarria collection.)

The Rodeo-Vallejo Ferry Company's only boat was the *Aven J. Hanford*, built in 1922 utilizing the engine from the destroyer USS *Farragut*. That same year, the Rodeo-Vallejo went out of business, and the *Aven J. Hanford* went to the Golden Gate Ferry. On April 22, 1927, she was renamed *Golden City* but two days later was rammed and sunk. (Bill Knorp collection.)

The *Golden State* was built in 1926 for Golden Gate Ferry as an auto carrier. Initially, like the other GGF boats, she was painted golden yellow, but after the SP merger, she was in white. In her later life on Puget Sound she was renamed *Kehloken*. (James Carpenter photograph; Bill Knorp collection.)

At midnight on Friday, February 28, 1941, the *Eureka*, long a mainstay for the Northwestern Pacific Railroad, made her final NWP revenue run. The next week she became a Southern Pacific boat, running between the Ferry Building and the Oakland Mole until retirement in 1956. (Bill Knorp collection.)

Although Ferry Building–Oakland Mole commuter ferries were long gone, SP ferry services for transcontinental trains continued the ferry legacy until 1958, retaining their warm spots in the hearts of those who had ridden them. Late into the 1950s, San Francisco postcards featured the ferryboats. (Trimble collection.)

The *San Leandro* was built in 1923 in Los Angeles for the Key System. On July 30, 1958, under the command of Capt. Richard Thomas, she made the last revenue run for the Southern Pacific and ended 89 years of ferryboating from the Oakland Mole. (Bill Knorp collection.)

In 1903, Francis M. Smith formed the Key Route, later the Key System, by merging Alameda County's independent street railways into a transit conglomerate of streetcars, interurbans, and ferries, which were served by the Key Pier, extending 3.2 miles over Oakland's shoals. (Trimble collection.)

The orange Key Route interurban trains went onto the pier and right into the ferry terminal, with an elegant exterior and interior. The Key Route even sold its own postcards, which were inexpensive stationary and even cheaper advertising. (Trimble collection.)

Pictured from left to right in this early view of the Key Pier, a string of interurban cars and ferryboats—the *Yerba Buena I*, the *Fernwood*, and the *Claremont*—are visible. The orange paint on the Key's ferries did not make them very photogenic due to the quality of film at the time. (Trimble collection.)

The Key Route's electric interurbans arrived on the Key Pier, while inside the terminal, passengers walked through the waiting room at the left to board the ferries. The waiting room was typical of the era, complete with potted palms. The trains were also painted Key Route orange. (Trimble collection.)

Past the pilothouse and the hurricane deck of the *Yerba Buena* is the Key Route's *San Francisco* at the Key Pier in the early 1920s. Built in 1905, the *San Francisco* went to the Golden Gate Ferry in 1924 to become the *Golden Dawn*. She was retired in 1937. (Trimble collection.)

The Key Route ferryboat *Fernwood*, fifth of the line, entered service on February 2, 1908, reflecting the growing popularity of the new company. The slightly shorter route and faster boats with their propeller drive were effective competition to the Southern Pacific. (Trimble collection.)

The Key Route ferries were strictly for passengers, although some were rebuilt as auto ferries under later ownerships. The *Yerba Buena I*, coming into port in the 1910s, became the Golden Gate Ferry *Harry E. Speas* in 1924 and, in 1927, was renamed the *Golden Coast*. (Trimble collection.)

The *Claremont* joined the Key Route fleet on March 14, 1907. In 1924, she was sold to the Golden Gate Ferry to be rebuilt as the auto ferry *Golden Way*. She was retired in 1937, when the Bay Bridge opened for motor-vehicle traffic. (Trimble collection.)

The *Hayward's* propellers are reversing to reduce speed as she moves into her Ferry Building slip during the 1920s. People crowd the forward of both the maindeck and the cabin deck in order to be among the first off the ferry, right behind the baggage cart. (Trimble collection.)

The Key System ferries were usually in the forefront of ferry technology; the *Hayward* was no exception. The restaurants aboard the Key's boats were notorious for their fine food, including their famous Key Route Hash and Key Route Coffee, a special blend served in chinaware, not paper or plastic. (Trimble collection.)

The late historian-photographer Bert H. Ward took this portrait of the Key System's San Francisco–bound *Yerba Buena II*, passing the Northwestern Pacific Railroad's *Tamalpais*, which is heading

for Sausalito from the Ferry Building. (The late Bert H. Ward photograph; Trimble collection.)

The Key Route's *Peralta* was a hard-luck boat. Built in 1927 in Oakland, she had a series of mishaps until May 6, 1933, when she was destroyed in the Key Pier fire. Her remains went to the Black Ball Line on Puget Sound to be completely rebuilt as the *Kalakala*. (From the late Charles A. Smallwood, Trimble collection.)

After the 1933 fire, the Key System used a prefabricated steel building for a terminal, as work had already begun for the Bay Bridge alongside the pier, now the site of the Bridge Toll Plaza. The *Yerba Buena II* is at left with the *San Leandro* at right. (Trimble collection.)

In the Key System days, the *San Leandro*, built in 1922, was the last word in San Francisco Bay ferries—steel hull, screw drive, and turboelectric engine. She retained her handsome proportions until the end, regardless of ownership. (Trimble collection.)

The Key System deferred to the Bay Bridge and ended its commute ferries in 1939. The Key continued to run ferries to the Golden Gate International Exposition on Treasure Island, augmenting its navy by leasing three ferries from the SP, including the *Piedmont*. (The late Bert H. Ward photograph; Trimble collection.)

During the 1939 season of the Golden Gate International Exposition on Treasure Island, the Key System operated ferries both to San Francisco and to Oakland. To meet patronage demands, the *Piedmont* was one of three Southern Pacific ferries leased by the Key System. In this picture, the *Piedmont* is tied up at the Key Pier, a strange place for a SP ferry—unless pained in Key System orange!

The *Ocean Wave* was built in 1891 for the Ilwaco Railway and Transportation Company on the Columbia River. Towed to Richmond in 1899, she began service for the Atchison, Topeka, and Santa Fe in 1900, taking rail passengers between Richmond and San Francisco. (Vallejo Naval and Historical Museum.)

The *San Pedro* was built in 1911 for the Santa Fe. During World War I, AT&SF trains went to the Oakland Mole with the Santa Fe boats used as extras. Richmond service resumed from 1919 until 1933 when AT&SF trains reverted to the Oakland Mole. (Jim Carpenter photograph; Bill Knorp collection.)

The Key System bought the *San Pedro* in 1938 and renamed her *Treasure Island* to take construction workers to her namesake for the World's Fair. She was in fair service from 1939 to 1940, then went to the Martinez-Benicia but was unsuitable. In 1942, she "joined" the U.S. Navy, becoming USS *North* (YFB 46) and a barracks for ammunition workers. (Trimble collection.)

By the late 1920s, automobile growth had reached such proportions that serious plans were made to bridge the San Francisco Bay. This view from Yerba Buena Island shows the Bay Bridge being built while the ferries are still running, albeit on borrowed time. (Trimble collection.)

From 1942 until April 1945, the *Yerba Buena* was in U.S. Maritime Commission service. She was then transferred to the Army Transportation Corps, moving troops between San Francisco, Oakland, and Pittsburg. For a while, she was renamed the *Ernie Pyle*, reverting back to *Yerba Buena* in 1946. The *San Leandro*, also in government service, is in the background. (Trimble collection.)

Tucked amidst the flora of Mandeville Island in the Sacramento–San Joaquin River Delta lies what remains of a once-proud ferryboat. The stern pilothouse is gone, along with most clues by which to identify her. It is very sad. (Paul Wamsley photograph; Trimble collection.)

Two

FERRIES OF THE NORTH BAY

Ferryboats serving the North Bay counties of Marin, Sonoma, and Solano carried just about anything needing waterborne transport in the years predating the bridges, including livestock, automobiles, trucks, buses, hearses, railroad freight cars, mail, express packages, commuters, hikers, vacationers, and both men and women consigned by law to residency in San Quentin Prison.

It should not be considered insignificant that the first of the San Francisco Bay's ferry services originated in the North Bay and that the region continues to not only have ferries but also the last family owned ferry line in the Bay Area (discussed in Chapter Four).

The North Bay ferries even found their way into American literature, for it was the ramming and sinking of the ferry *San Rafael* by the *Sausalito* that formed the basis for Jack London's novel *The Sea Wolf.*

The Saucelito Land and Ferry Company organized in 1868 to develop Sausalito real estate. Absent regular ferry services, SL&F bought the nine-year-old *Princess* to run from Meiggs Wharf in San Francisco to Sausalito's Princess Street, named for the ferryboat. The *Princess* was laid up in 1874 and dismantled in 1891. (NWPRRHS Archives; Stindt collection.)

Sausalito's waterfront, *c.* 1875, shows the Saucelito Land and Ferry Company's *Petaluma*, built in 1857 and renamed *Petaluma of Saucelito* in 1875. In 1877, she was rebuilt as the *Tamalpais I*. The steamer at left is Charles Minturn's *Contra Costa*, no longer an active ferry but used occasionally for excursions. (NWPRRHS Archives; Stindt collection.)

This view of the North Pacific Coast Railroad's (NPC) ferry landing at Sausalito shows the *San Rafael* at left and the *Tamalpais I* at right. At center is the *Bay City*, probably on loan from the SP as a relief boat, a familiar duty for the *Bay City*. (NWPRRHS Archives; Stindt collection.)

The Northwestern Pacific Railroad was formed in 1907 by merging seven railroads, one of which was the standard-gauge California Northwestern, nee San Francisco and North Pacific, which also ran ferries between Tiburon, pictured here in April 1884, and San Francisco. The *James M. Donahue* is under steam while the *Tiburon* at lower left is idle. (NWPRRHS Archives.)

Before World War II, the area of Sausalito where tourists now throng was a railroad yard and ferry depot for the NWP, an SP subsidiary. Here interurbans from San Rafael and Manor as well as steam trains from Eureka, the Russian River, and the Sonoma Valley met the San Francisco–bound ferries. (Trimble collection.)

The first thing to greet passengers upon arrival at Sausalito was the ferry terminal, through which people walked to board either a NWP local electric or steam train headed for the Russian River, the Sonoma Valley, or Eureka, some 250 miles north. (Trimble collection.)

Outside the ferry terminal, NWP passengers needed only a few steps to get to their trains. Today the railroad and the steam ferries are gone from Sausalito, although ferries of the Golden Gate Bridge, Highway and Transportations District dock nearby. (Trimble collection.)

A major stimulus for the NWP ferry business was the Mount Tamalpais and Muir Woods Railroad (right), running from the NWP Mill Valley depot to the summit of Mount Tamalpais. To get to the "mountain railroad," as locals called it, one took an interurban (left) from Sausalito. (Trimble collection.)

In 1929, the NWP ordered new rolling stock for its electric system. Alas, the automobile had taken hold, and these cars were later to run longer in Southern California than in Marin County. Here a train approaches Pine Point en route to Sausalito and a rendezvous with the ferryboats. (The late Charles A. Smallwood; Trimble collection.)

The Oakland ferries originally docked at San Francisco's Davis Street Wharf, but by 1875, increasing ferryboat business warranted a new terminal at the foot of Market Street. In 1896, construction began for a more commodious Ferry Building on the same site, and Market Street's cable cars used a temporary turntable. When the project ended in 1898, the cable cars reverted to their original turntable location. (Courtesy NWPRRHS Archives.)

The *James M. Donahue* was built for the SF&NP in 1875 to run from Donahue Landing to San Francisco. While single enders were faster than double-enders, they lost time turning around to begin a new trip. The *James M. Donahue* went to her reward in 1924. (Trimble collection.)

Sister ships *San Rafael* and *Saucelito* were built in New York in 1877, disassembled, and then reassembled in California. On a foggy November 30, 1901, the *San Rafael* was rammed and sunk off Alcatraz Island by the *Sausalito*, losing several lives and inspiring Jack London's novel *The Sea Wolf*. In 1921, the anchor on the liner *Matsonia I* snagged the *San Rafael's* walking beam, all that was ever salvaged from the ship. (Bill Knorp collection.)

Steamers such as the *San Rafael* were anything but "green" by today's standards—lumbermen's axes felled countless trees to build them, they burned low-grade coal (before converting to burning crude oil), garbage from the restaurants was routinely tossed overboard, and the "heads" emptied directly into the bay. (NWPRRHS Archives; Stindt collection.)

This is perhaps the only known image of the *Saucelito*, sister ship to the *San Rafael*. The *Saucelito* was destroyed by fire in 1884. Saucelito, the original Spanish spelling, was used until 1887, when the Anglicized form, Sausalito, was adopted by the post office. (NWPRRHS Archives.)

Although the *Tiburon* was not built until 1884, her vertical engine had been erected by San Francisco's Union Iron Works in 1860, then stored, unused. Following World War I, the *Tiburon* was designated the NWP's first automobile ferry, making the 3:55 p.m. run to Sausalito from the Ferry Building. (Bill Knorp collection, Trimble collection.)

Upon entering SF&NP service in 1890, the versatile *Ukiah* was primarily a car float, for on her maindeck were tracks for 12 railcars. Alternatively, she could carry 85 automobiles and was rated to carry 1,000 foot passengers. (NWPRRHS Archives.)

Ordinarily, ferrying freight cars on the *Ukiah* was routine, but even the best of ferryboats can have a bad day, as this photograph shows. The crew has lashed down the errant freight cars, so presumably all was not lost that day. (NWPRRHS Archives; Stindt collection.)

This shows the 1901 launching of the NPC's *Tamalpais II* at the Union Iron Works in San Francisco. Despite a 2,100 horsepower engine, she could not make her designated speed, so she was lengthened by 15 feet at each end, solving the problem. The *Tammy* was the NWP's only steel-hulled double-ender. (NWPRRHS Archives; Stindt collection.)

This book would not be complete without this fine image from the camera of the late Wilbur C. Whittaker, showing the *Tamalpais* heaving into the Ferry Building with the *Yerba Buena* just behind her as the *Berkeley* heads for Oakland. (The late Wilbur C. Whittaker photograph; Trimble collection.)

The *Tamalpais* arrives at the Ferry Building in 1923. Certainly one of the most graceful of the NWP fleet, she was built by the Union Iron Works in San Francisco in 1901. Her last run, on February 28, 1941, marked the finale of Northwestern Pacific Railroad ferryboats. (Bill Knorp collection.)

Due to Southern Pacific ownership of the NWP, it was not unusual for NWP ferries to receive major repairs or overhauls at the SP shipyard in Oakland. Here the NWP's *Sausalito* and the SP's *Encinal* are pictured in the early 1930s. (Bill Knorp collection.)

The *Sausalito* is tied up at the pier in Tiburon in the early 1930s after getting a new paint job. The NWP serviced its ferries at Tiburon, and it was at Tiburon Shops where repairs were made to the railroad's rolling stock. (Bill Knorp collection.)

Between 1894 and 1934, the *Sausalito* served the NPC, the North Shore Railroad, and the NWP. Since 1934, she has been home to a private rod-and-gun club near the Antioch Bridge. This picture was taken on August 1, 1926, in Sausalito by Mike Guilholm, photographer for the NWP. (Mike Guilholm photograph; Bill Knorp collection.)

The late Dr. Thomas H. Snead, a Marin County dentist, made this working model of the *Sausalito*. On display at the Marin History Museum in San Rafael, the model shows the NWP livery of black stack, red walking beam, orange paddle wheels, and green hull. (Bill Knorp collection.)

This 1922 photograph of the *Sausalito* arriving at the Ferry Building from Marin shows foot passengers on both the cabin deck and the maindeck, along with automobiles. The NWP accepted automobile traffic, but only grudgingly, feeling that automobiles were a detriment to the railroad business. (Bill Knorp collection.)

Marin County ferryboat aficionado Dr. Thomas H. Snead took this photograph of the *Cazadero* in the 1930s. Atop her hurricane deck is the walking beam, which transferred energy from the piston to the eccentric shaft turning the paddle wheels. (The late Dr. Thomas H. Snead photograph; Bill Knorp collection.)

NORTHWESTERN PACIFIC RAILROAD CO'S FERRY STEAMER "CAZADERO" UNDER REPAIR AT MOORE DRYDOCK COMPANY'S SHIPYARD, OAKLAND, CALIFORNIA, JANUARY 26, 1923. 3125

In 1922, the *Cazadero*'s walking beam ran amok, ripping a huge gash from the hurricane deck through the fiddley, which required extensive repairs. The only good news was that a photographer left an excellent cross-section view of a San Francisco Bay ferryboat. (NWPRRHS Archives.)

The *Cazadero* was built in 1903 for the North Shore Railroad, which came into the NWP in 1907. As built, the *Cazadero* had a permanent list to port and had to be reballasted, slightly reducing her rated speed. She lasted until 1942 when she was scrapped. (The late Wilbur C. Whittaker photograph; Trimble collection.)

The year is 1923, and the *Eureka*, newly rebuilt from the *Ukiah*, arrives at San Francisco's Ferry Building still using the old A-frame, walking beam, and paddle wheels from her days as the *Ukiah*. Most of her hull and all of her superstructure are new, however. (Bill Knorp collection.)

NORTHWESTERN PACIFIC FERRY STR. "EUREKA" WALKING BEAM FOR MAIN ENGINE CONSTRUCTED BY THE MOORE DRY-DOCK COMPANY, OAKLAND, CAL. JULY 19, 1926. 3471

In 1926, the *Eureka* received a new walking beam made by the Moore Drydock Company in Oakland. The size of the walking beam may be measured in feet and inches, but when compared to the machinist in this picture, it becomes truly massive. (Trimble collection.)

FERRY STR. "EUREKA" RECEIVING NEWLY CONSTRUCTED WALKING BEAM.
THE MOORE DRY-DOCK CO., OAKLAND, CALIF., JULY 24, 1926.   3502

The huge crane hoisting the new walking beam to the A-frame on the *Eureka's* hurricane deck tells it all—size! The *Eureka* was the largest passenger ferry on San Francisco Bay. At 2,420 tons, she could carry 2,300 passengers and 90 automobiles. (Trimble collection.)

This unusual picture shows the year-old *Eureka* at the NWP servicing dock in Tiburon getting her maindeck windows repaired. Ferries usually went in for repairs for about two weeks. The NWP borrowed the *Oakland* from the SP to maintain schedules. (Bill Knorp collection.)

The *Eureka* served the Northwestern Pacific until 1941, when she was transferred to the Southern Pacific for the Oakland–San Francisco run, serving until September 30, 1956, when a damaged crankshaft pin caused her retirement. She is preserved today as the last of America's wooden-hulled, walking-beam vessels. (The late Wilbur C. Whittaker photograph; Trimble collection.)

The 97-foot steamer *Requa*, the smallest of the NWP ferries, ran between Tiburon, Belvedere, and Sausalito. Reportedly built in 1909 for Nevada millionaire Mark Requa, she went to the NWP that year, replacing the *James M. Donahue*. In 1911, she burned to her waterline and was rebuilt as the gasoline-powered *Marin*, serving until 1933, when she was replaced by a bus service. The *Marin* was scrapped in 1935. (Fred Codoni Collection.)

The ungainly *Lagunitas* was built in 1903 for the North Shore Railroad to ferry freight cars. For some reason, her wooden hull was never sheathed with copper plating, allowing marine life to use it for a smorgasbord. By 1917, she was a nautical basket case and was retired. (NWPRRHS Archives; Stindt collection.)

The *Lagunitas* had little to recommend her. Her wooden hull was unsheathed, she could only hold 10 freight cars compared to a dozen on the *Ukiah*, and her poppet-valve engine only had 400 horsepower. It was said that the slow sternwheeler once lost a race with Alcatraz Island! (NWPRRHS Archives; Stindt collection.)

The NWP freight slip at Tiburon was designed to bring freight cars on and off ferries, and later barges, which were moved by the tugboat *Tiger*, built for the North Pacific Coast Railroad. In this 1900 picture, *Tiger* is pushing NPC Transfer Barge No. 2. The sidewheel tug was scrapped in 1917, at the age of 42. (NWPRRHS Archives.)

The Espee's *Oakland* seems out of place, arriving in Sausalito on a NWP run in 1938. However, SP ferries often filled in while the NWP ferries were being repaired. Then again, in *Oakland's* former life as the *Chrysopolis*, she may have made a trip or two to Marin County. (The late Bert Ward photograph; Bill Knorp collection.)

Launching of
FERRY-BOAT "MENDOCINO"
APRIL 14, 1927

BETHLEHEM SHIPBUILDING CORP. LTD
UNION PLANT   POTRERO WORKS
                                   S.F. CALIF.
MERINETTI LAKE
of the
Yokayo Tribe of Indians
SPONSOR

The launching of the M. V. *Mendocino* signified the NWP's acquiescence to the auto-ferry business, believing that cars would take business away from the trains. They were right, for the Golden Gate Bridge did them all in, and the *Mendocino* went to Puget Sound to become the *Nisqually*. (NWPRRHS Archives.)

After long resisting auto carriers, the NWP built three in 1927, including the 2,467 ton, diesel-electric *Mendocino*, to take cars between Sausalito and San Francisco's Hyde Street Pier. Two years later, the three went to Southern Pacific–Golden Gate Ferries, Limited. (Trimble collection.)

The NWP's three sister ship auto ferries only lasted two years in NWP livery, going to Southern Pacific–Golden Gate Ferries in 1929. Only eight years later, the *Redwood Empire* went to Puget Sound, becoming the *Quinault*. (NWPRRHS Archives)

The 1929 merger forming the Southern Pacific–Golden Gate Ferries, Limited included the three nearly new NWP car ferries, the *Santa Rosa*, *Mendocino*, and *Redwood Empire*. The *Santa Rosa* went to Puget Sound and was renamed the *Enetai* in 1938. (NWPRRHS Archives.)

This view is of the auto-ferry dock at Sausalito, where the ferryboat at right is loading for another trip to San Francisco's Hyde Street Pier. Unfortunately the signs and apron apparatus have obstructed the ferries' identities. (NWPRRHS Archives; Stindt collection.)

The demarcation between ferries and riverboats was not absolute; the 1868 sternwheeler *Caroline* served as both. Owned and operated by Capt. William G. Leale from 1892 to 1917, when burned at Sausalito, the *Caroline* made regular trips to San Quentin Prison with supplies and visitors from San Francisco's mail dock. Parolees acted as crewmen. (Trimble collection.)

Because the partners could not agree whether the Richmond–San Rafael Ferries should be painted barn red or white, the boats were repainted red and white in alternate years well into the 1920s. The chain-link logo on the *City of Richmond* represented the company's namesake cities. (San Francisco Maritime NHP.)

The Richmond–San Rafael Ferry's *City of San Rafael* was, in 1924, the last sidewheeler built on the bay. In 1938, she went into standby status. In 1943, the sidewheeler was sold to Martinez-Benicia Ferry, serving until 1956, when she was beached in Sausalito for housing. (San Francisco Maritime NHP.)

The Richmond–San Rafael Ferry's *Sonoma Valley* began as the Key Route's *San Jose* in 1903. In 1919, Six Minute Ferry rebuilt her into an auto ferry. In 1922, Six Minute Ferry was sold to Rodeo-Vallejo Ferry. In 1927, the *San Jose* went to the R-SR, becoming the *Sonoma Valley*. She was junked in 1947. (Trimble collection.)

Looking down at the Castro Point terminal of the Richmond–San Rafael Ferry, *c.* 1942, the *City of Richmond* and the *City of San Rafael* are on standby status. Docked at the left, approaching from Point San Quentin and in the distance, nearing San Quentin, are the three former SP boats, *El Paso*, *Klamath*, and *Russian River*. (San Francisco Maritime NHP B12.3689.)

In 1915, the Key Route extended its McDonald Avenue streetcar line in Richmond to the Blake Brothers quarry and the Richmond–San Rafael Ferry pier. In this 1933 photograph, the streetcar is returning from the Castro Point ferry terminal on its way to Hayward, then California's longest streetcar line. (Trimble collection.)

This ferry began as the WP's *Edward T. Jeffrey* in 1913, was renamed the *Feather River* in 1930, was sold to the SP and renamed *Sierra Nevada* in 1933, was leased to the Key System from 1939 to 1941 and to the U.S. Maritime Commission from 1942 to 1945, and was acquired by Richmond–San Rafael Ferry in 1947. (Alvon J. Thoman photograph; Trimble collection.)

Once the ferry was secured, an apron was lowered from the dock to the maindeck, allowing vehicles to drive onto the *Russian River* regardless of high or low tides. A brace of Chevys lead the way in this 1956 photograph. (Alvon J. Thoman photograph; Trimble collection.)

The last years of the Richmond–San Rafael Ferry saw the company using secondhand vessels made surplus because of the Bay Bridge, among them the *Russian River*, formerly the SP ferry *New Orleans*. All R-SRF ferryboats were retired in 1956. (Trimble collection.)

The *El Paso* off-loads a big Cadillac and an even bigger truck at Point San Quentin on July 15, 1954. Over time, the R-SRF's patronage included cars, pedestrians, and even cattle, not to mention some of California's more contumacious recalcitrants, bound for durance vile at nearby San Quentin Prison. (Alvon J. Thoman photograph; Trimble collection.)

With their cars parked safely on the maindeck, passengers on the port side of the cabin deck of the *Klamath*, bound for Castro Point on the Contra Costa side, enjoy a leisurely summer day in 1956, well before today's air-quality regulations. (Alvon J. Thoman photograph; Trimble collection.)

The Richmond–San Rafael's *Klamath* steams westerly from Castro Point on May 20, 1956. In the background is the Richmond–San Rafael Bridge, which, like other publicly financed roadways, meant the end of privately owned ferryboat systems. (Alvon J. Thoman photograph; Trimble collection.)

In the early morning of August 25, 1956, at Castro Point, the *El Paso* fires up in her berth, the *Klamath* approaches from Point San Quentin on the Marin side, and the *Sierra Nevada* is on standby. Six days later, their fires would be extinguished for good. (Alvon J. Thoman photograph; Trimble collection.)

This rotting hulk on Sausalito's waterfront in 1980 was once the *Charles Van Damme*, flagship of the R-SRF. In Sausalito, she was first a nightclub and restaurant called The Ark, then Juanita's Galley. Other ferries beached at Sausalito were the *City of Richmond*, *City of Seattle*, *Issaquah*, and *Vallejo*. (Trimble photograph.)

The *New World* steamed from New York to California in 1850 and worked the Golden State's rivers for a decade. She then ran on Puget Sound and the Columbia River, returning in 1869 for the California Pacific Railroad ferry between South Vallejo and San Francisco until broken up in 1879. (Vallejo Naval and Historical Museum.)

The riverboat *Herald* rates inclusion because her run from Napa to San Francisco via the Napa River and Vallejo competed with the *Sunol* and the Monticello boats. Completion of the SP rails through the Napa Valley in 1905 caused the 27-year-old sternwheeler's retirement. (Vallejo Naval and Historical Museum.)

The *H. J. Corcoran*, built in 1898, was one of the fastest steamers in California, finishing off the Aden Brothers *Sunol* and forcing the Hatch Brothers Steamship Company to bring in faster boats. After a collision with the *Seminole* in 1913, she was rebuilt as the *Crockett* and sold to C and H Sugar Company. (San Francisco Maritime NHP P82-100.9.)

Pictured at Mare Island Strait in 1885, the *Julia*, built in 1870, served both the Central and Southern Pacific as the bay's first oil burner. She was destroyed in a boiler explosion on February 27, 1888. Ferrymen said they should have stayed with coal, although later ferries burned oil without problems. (Vallejo Naval and Historical Museum.)

The Espee used the former South Pacific Coast ferry *Bay City* on its Vallejo–Vallejo Junction run, pictured here. The SP abandoned this operation with the opening of the Carquinez Bridge in 1927, and in 1929, the 51-year-old *Bay City* was dismantled. (Vallejo Naval and Historical Museum.)

Aden Brothers built the 135-foot *Sunol* in 1890 for direct service between central Vallejo and San Francisco, taking three hours and 45 minutes each way. After 1905, the *Sunol* was freight only until 1913, and in 1924, she was sold to the Leslie Salt Company. She was vacated in 1946 on the Napa River and disintegrated. (Vallejo Naval and Historical Museum.)

The *Monticello* was built in 1892 in Ballard, Washington, for Zepheniah J. Hatch, who brought her to San Francisco in 1895. With his brother, Zepheniah formed the Hatch Brothers Steamship Company, which quickly offered effective competition on the Vallejo–San Francisco route. (Vallejo Naval and Historical Museum.)

In this 1906 photograph, the Monticello Steamship Company ferries from San Francisco are met at Vallejo's Maine Street Wharf by the electric trains of the Vallejo, Benicia, and Napa Valley Railroad. The two railcars at the right once ran on the Park and Ocean Railroad in San Francisco. (From the late Randolph Brandt, Trimble collection.)

In 1927, the Monticello ferries were modernized for end loading of automobiles, and new dock facilities were built at the Georgia Street pier. The railroad, now simply called the Napa Valley Route, continued to meet the ferries as seen here in April 1937. (From the late Stephen D. Maguire, Trimble collection.)

The Napa Valley Route took the mail contract from the Southern Pacific in 1927, resulting in the Monticello ferries becoming U.S. mail carriers and providing needed income in the face of increasing automobile competition. This photograph was taken in Napa in 1936. (Trimble collection.)

The *General Frisbie*, built in 1890 for Hatch Brothers, was a speedy craft and won her share of races. Racing was officially forbidden by the ferries' ownerships, and a skipper could get five demerits if caught. Of course, he could get 10 demerits if he lost the race! (Vallejo Naval and Historical Museum.)

STEAMER "ARROW" FOR SAN FRANCISCO, MARE ISLAND NAVY YARD AND VALLEJO, CAL.

The *Arrow*, built in 1903 on Puget Sound, came to Hatch Brothers in 1904, when the company reorganized as the Monticello Steamship Company. She was retired and vacated at San Francisco's Hunters Point in 1929. The Monticello ferries' time between Vallejo and San Francisco was just under two hours. (Vallejo Naval and Historical Museum.)

The 2,189-ton *Napa Valley* was the first locally built Monticello boat, built in 1910 by Bethlehem Steel Company with a triple-expansion engine of 2,600 horsepower. In the background, during *Napa Valley*'s maiden run are the *El Capitan* and the navy launch USS *Pinafor*. (Vallejo Naval and Historical Museum.)

Built as the sternwheeler *Mountain Queen* at The Dalles, Oregon, in 1877, this vessel became the sidewheeler *Sehome* in 1889. In 1909, she came to the Monticello line and in 1914 was converted to screw drive. In 1918, she was rammed and sunk by the *General Frisbie*, the Monticello's only serious accident. (Vallejo Naval and Historical Museum.)

The *Asbury Park* and the *Napa Valley* appear together at Vallejo. Despite the time consumed turning around to begin their trips, the Monticello ferries easily made up the time, finishing the 30-mile run in just under two hours, tides and fogs permitting. (Vallejo Naval and Historical Museum.)

The speedy *Asbury Park* was built in 1903 in Philadelphia. On her inaugural run for Monticello on November 20, 1919, her wash broke every mooring in the Mare Island channel, causing the Mare Island commandant to lodge a complaint. It would be the first of many more. (Vallejo Naval and Historical Museum.)

THE PALATIAL STEAMER "CITY OF SACRAMENTO", VALLEJO—SAN FRANCISCO SERVICE.

This postcard view is of the *City of Sacramento* in original configuration. When rebuilt as auto ferries, the Monticello boats lost their graceful exterior in favor of more expeditious loading and off-loading of automobiles; however, business was business. (Vallejo Naval and Historical Museum.)

The Monticello ferries' growing popularity demanded yet another boat, so the *Florida* of Baltimore's Old Bay Line was acquired and renamed the *Calistoga*. Later rebuilt to carry automobiles, she was scrapped in 1941 after 34 years of service. (Vallejo Naval and Historical Museum.)

The interiors of the Monticello vessels were not spartan by a long shot! This view of the *Calistoga* is looking aft and below from the texas (see glossary) down to the newsstand and the cabin deck. All Monticello boats had saloons, which helped keep the company in the black. (Vallejo Naval and Historical Museum.)

The Monticello Steamship Company had an early version of park 'n' ride, as some Solano County patrons preferred leaving their cars in Vallejo while ferrying to San Francisco. Monticello boats offered everything: restaurants, barbershops, newsstands, washrooms, smoking rooms, and time to relax. A round-trip ticket cost 75¢. (Vallejo Naval and Historical Museum.)

The double-stacker *Asbury Park* became the single-stacker *City of Sacramento* when rebuilt in 1925 for larger crowds and car-ferry services. In 1927, the Golden Gate Ferry bought the Monticello Steamship Company for $2 million, a hefty sum in those days! (Vallejo Naval and Historical Museum.)

Golden Gate Ferries bought the Monticello Steamship Company for $2 million in 1927 and rebuilt the *Napa Valley* (above), the *City of Sacramento*, and the *Calistoga* to carry automobiles. The *Napa Valley* held 100 cars and carried passengers on her texas. In 1942, she went to Puget Sound, becoming the *Malahat*. (Trimble collection.)

The Mare Island Naval Shipyard opened in 1854, and service to Vallejo began in 1855 using government steamers *Huron* and *Ion*. The Mare Island Ferry Company began in the late 1860s with the sidewheeler *Lizzie*, followed by the *Mare Island* in 1870. Apparently the *Lizzie* did not last beyond 1879. (Vallejo Naval and Historical Museum.)

Originally the *Vallejo* had a single wheelhouse situated amidships on the hurricane deck. Later the ferry was rebuilt with twin wheelhouses. The *Vallejo* served for 69 years until 1948, probably the record for San Francisco Bay ferries. (Vallejo Naval and Historical Museum.)

The Mare Island Ferry sold the *Mare Island* and acquired the *Vallejo* in 1879. It took only a few minutes to cross the Mare Island Strait, and the ferry was packed with civilian workers during the morning and afternoon rush. The *Vallejo* was one of the few ferries that allowed passengers on the hurricane deck. (Vallejo Naval and Historical Museum.)

The Mare Island Ferry's 133-foot *Ellen* was truly a hometown ferryboat, having been built in Vallejo in 1883, having served Vallejo until she was condemned in 1915 (save for one month with the Richmond–San Rafael Ferry), and having been brought back to Vallejo to be broken up in 1919. Her home port was always Vallejo. (Vallejo Naval and Historical Museum.)

The U.S. Navy also operated launches between Mare Island and Vallejo, and in this 1920s photograph, sailors and U.S. Marines are going "on the beach" at Vallejo, with the Monticello's *General Frisbie* and *Asbury Park* in the background. Will the Marine MP be a busy man patrolling Vallejo's notorious Georgia Street? (Vallejo Naval and Historical Museum.)

Among the more diminutive of the San Francisco Bay ferries was the 114.4-foot, 288-ton *Issaquah*. Built in 1914 for Puget Sound service, she was purchased by the Rodeo-Vallejo Ferry Company in 1918, by the Martinez-Benicia Ferry in 1927, then by the Mare Island Ferry in 1943. She was vacated in 1948. (Trimble collection.)

The *Issaquah*, affectionately called *The Squash*, had a lot of mileage and even more history. In this July 17, 1948, photograph at the Georgia Street wharf in Vallejo, she is "finished with engines" and bears no livery, and her days as a ferryboat are over. (Trimble collection.)

The *Issaquah* was beached in Sausalito in 1948, becoming housing for local artists. Too many years of neglect brought her to this shameful state, pictured here on March 1, 1980. Shortly after this photograph was taken, she was destroyed in a clearance project, an end the old "Squash" did not deserve. (Trimble photograph.)

This shall be the book's mystery photograph. The former Mare Island Ferry *Vallejo* was photographed on June 17, 1948, bearing the name *Magdalena* on her signboards. There are no maritime records of any such vessel of that name, and it appears that *Magdalena* is fictitious. But why? (Trimble collection.)

Three

ACROSS THE CARQUINEZ

The Carquinez Strait is actually only the western portion of a body of water feeding into San Francisco Bay, but for the purposes of this chapter, it shall be construed to include the strait itself, Suisun Bay, and the confluence of the Sacramento and San Joaquin Rivers, which together separate Solano County on the north from Contra Costa County to the south.

While none of the ferryboat operations on the Carquinez had large fleets or were in and of themselves major commuter operations, two of them have earned their places in maritime history for having the largest ferryboats in the world and the nation's only interurban ferryboat. Further significance is attached to the latter, as she was powered by the world's largest distillate engine.

All but one were under private ownership, the exception being the Martinez-Benicia Ferry, which for a while was owned by the City of Martinez and later by the State of California.

These operations may have been minor in the larger scale of things, but it nonetheless took a slew of bridges and the U.S. Coast Guard to put them out of business.

The Southern Pacific ferry *Amador* is docked at Vallejo Junction, halfway between Crockett and Rodeo, taking transfers from the Sacramento-bound local train at right. From Vallejo Junction, the *Amador* will steam to South Vallejo, site of the California Maritime Academy, and then to Vallejo, about another mile. (John V. Robinson collection.)

Before 1876, Central Pacific's San Francisco–bound patrons transferred to riverboats in Sacramento. The CPRR absorbed the Vallejo-Sacramento California Pacific Railroad that year and extended its rails to Benicia. In 1879, the train ferry *Solano* was built to bring the trains across the Carquinez Strait to Port Costa. Westbound Train No. 21, the *St. Louis Express*, is shown here being off-loaded. (Trimble collection.)

The *Solano* had three tracks on her deck, and while she and the *Contra Costa* were primarily used for transferring trains, they also carried foot passengers across the Carquinez. Here deckhands are securing the train as the skipper surveys the scene from the pilothouse. (Contra Costa Historical Society.)

The *Solano* (left) and the *Contra Costa* (right) are berthed at Port Costa on the southern shore of the Carquinez Strait, awaiting another eastbound train. The *Solano*'s hogposts anchor a series of guys to strengthen the wooden hull against the weight of the trains, while the steel-hulled *Contra Costa* did not need them. (Southern Pacific photograph; Contra Costa Historical Society.)

It took a brace of two cylinder-compound steam engines to generate the 3,000 horsepower necessary to move the 4,483-ton *Contra Costa*. This giant ferry lasted only 16 years until the technology and financing became available to build the Southern Pacific's railroad bridge over the Carquinez. (Bill Knorp collection.)

In 1914, the SP built the *Contra Costa* to join the *Solano* on the Port Costa–Benicia run. The 4,483-ton *Contra Costa* was the world's largest ferryboat at the time—67.2 feet wide and 433 feet long. Onboard is SP Train No. 19, the *Pacific Limited* from Chicago, destined for the Oakland Mole. Note the list to port from the weight of the 110.45-ton locomotive. (Contra Costa Historical Society.)

The final revenue trip of the *Solano* was taken on October 15, 1930. As the massive ferry arrives at Port Costa, the train's passengers plus "all hands and the ship's cook" gather for the camera. The train ferries were replaced that day by a railroad bridge built by SP. (Contra Costa Historical Society.)

Sacramento Northern Railway predecessor, Oakland and Antioch, had planned to construct a bridge across the waters of the Carquinez but were unable to finance it. The "temporary" solution was the ferry *Bridgit* (Bridge-it), pictured here being built in 1913 at Moore and Scott Iron Works in Oakland. Also under construction at right is the *Edward T. Jeffrey* for the Western Pacific Railroad. The *Bridgit* was but a year old when destroyed by a fire. (San Francisco Maritime NHP; Scott Collection No. B4-4547N.)

To cross the Carquinez between Mallard and Chipps Islands, the Sacramento Northern Railway built the *Ramon* in 1915, replacing the *Bridgit*, which burned in 1914. They were America's only interurban train ferries and carried both passenger and freight trains. The *Ramon* was retired in 1954 when U.S. Coast Guard–mandated repairs were deemed too expensive by the SN. (The late Stephen D. Maguire, Trimble collection.)

SN No. *670* works a cut of freight cars onto the *Ramon* at Mallard in 1949. The flatcar is a "reacher" so the ferry won't have to bear the locomotive's weight. The *Ramon* was powered by a 600-horsepower, distillate, eight-cylinder engine, which was 46 feet long and weighed 1,000 pounds. At the time, it was the world's largest internal-combustion, electric-ignition engine. (Trimble collection.)

The Charles Van Damme, built in 1916 for the Richmond–San Rafael Ferry, served until laid up in 1939. In 1943, she was bought by the Martinez-Benicia Ferry, by then owned by the city of Martinez. This June 1950 picture shows the Charles Van Damme approaching Martinez, six years before State of California ownership and decertification by the U.S. Coast Guard. (San Francisco Maritime National Historic Park c12.2,580.)

Alice Hogarty Reiser poses on the maindeck of the City of Seattle, of Martinez-Benicia Ferry. Note the wheel chocks, provided in case an absent-minded motorist forgot to set the brakes. This 1888 sidewheeler was bereft of a cabin deck and was a mere 121.5 feet in length. (The late William R. Hogarty photograph; NWPRRHS Archives.)

In 1917, the Martinez-Benicia Ferry built the *City of Martinez* to complement the *City of Seattle*, but she was a disappointment from the start. Her displacement was so light that her paddle wheels failed to touch water. At 250 horsepower, she was neither especially fast nor noted for her looks and was condemned in 1936. (San Francisco Maritime NHP; B4.3147p.)

With the opening of the Carquinez Bridge in 1927, the Rodeo-Vallejo Ferry folded, and the *Issaquah* went to the Martinez-Benicia Ferry, her third owner. She would put in a stint for the Mare Island Ferry before retirement in 1948. (The late William R. Hogarty photograph; NWPRRHS Archives.)

While on standby in 1943, the *City of San Rafael* broke free of her moorings during a storm and wound up beached at Winehaven, near Point Molate. The U.S. Army bought her for salvage, but that same year sold her again, this time to the Martinez-Benicia Ferry, where she ran another 13 years. (Vallejo Naval and Historical Museum.)

The *Aven J. Hanford* was built in 1922 in Benicia for the Rodeo-Vallejo Ferry, which ceased operations upon the opening of the Carquinez Bridge in 1927. The *Aven J. Hanford* is pictured here at South Vallejo in 1922 with a line of U.S. Navy battleships in Rotten Row. (Vallejo Naval and Historical Museum.)

In 1919, the Association of Mare Island Employees bought the burned remains of the Key Route's *San Jose*, rebuilt her into an auto carrier, and started the Six Minute Ferry, named for the crossing time over the Carquinez from Morrow Cove to Crockett. A 1922 earth slide destroyed the Morrow Cove terminal and ended the Six Minute Ferry. (Contra Costa Historical Society.)

The Six Minute Ferry lasted less than four years, probably accounting for the slight number of photographs of the line, which competed with the Rodeo-Vallejo Ferry. The Morrow Cove wharf is now the site of the California Maritime Academy. The Six Minute Ferry's only boat, the *San Jose*, went to the Rodeo-Vallejo Ferry in 1922. (Vallejo Naval and Historical Museum.)

Four

TODAY'S FERRIES

Those of a nostalgic bent may argue that today's ferries are not ferryboats at all, but rather enclosed tour boats masquerading as ferries. However, they do ferry people and are included in the volume.

As traffic on the Golden Gate Bridge approached the capacity mark in 1970, the Golden Gate Bridge and Highway District sought relief by offering ferry services. The two became the Golden Gate Bridge, Highway and Transportation District, a rare case of a bridge reviving what it had once vanquished.

These and other contemporary ferry services connecting San Francisco with cities around the bay enjoy a good degree of customer loyalty in the belief that travel over water is preferable to fighting traffic congestion. Angel Island–Tiburon Ferry survives largely because if a bridge were to be built across Raccoon Strait, there would be no place to park all of the automobiles on the island, which is a state park.

Lastly, ferryboats that managed to avoid the scrappers' torches and ignominious beachings are also included. Whether they have become floating maritime museums or have been given new careers as floating office buildings, they offer lasting testimony to the elegance of a bygone age.

Moored at San Francisco's Pier No. 3 is the old *Santa Rosa* of the NWP, Golden Gate Ferry, Southern Pacific–Golden Gate Ferries, and later the *Enetai* of the Black Ball Line and Washington State Ferries. Fittingly, she is still in "maritime" service as the offices of Hornblower Cruises and Events. (Trimble photograph.)

As a floating maritime museum in balmy San Diego, the *Berkeley's* maindeck is fully enclosed, in contrast to her days on San Francisco Bay, when the deck was open to the fogs. While she may never steam again, her engines remain intact. (Trimble photograph.)

The *Eureka's* maindeck houses a collection of vintage cars and trucks reminiscent of the 1920s, when the NWP's car-carrying capacity was so limited that weekenders returning to San Francisco had to wait until past midnight to board a ferry. The only noticeable change today is a fence protecting these priceless relics from vandalism. (Trimble photograph.)

As pictured on the preserved *Eureka*, the pilothouse wheels are displayed, although the vessel used tillers, which controlled steering machines. At the right are the compass box, the brass speaking tube, the brass telegraph to the engine room, and the other appurtenances of the captain's domain, sans cuspidors. (Trimble photograph.)

The Angel Island–Tiburon Ferry is the only family owned ferry service on the bay. In this photograph, the custom built ferry *Angel Island* cuts across Raccoon Strait toward Angel Island State Park, one of the shortest of the bay's ferry routes. (Trimble photograph.)

The *Angel Island* eases alongside her dock at Tiburon, while a deckhand on the starboard bow readies to cast an eye splice over the pointed mooring post at the dock. Old Glory on the jack staff indicates that this was a breezy day on Raccoon Strait. (Trimble photograph.)

Capt. Maggie McDonogh is the fourth generation to work the family business and is the Angel Island–Tiburon Ferry's lone distaff skipper. Her dad, 91-year-old Capt. Milton McDonogh, spends his "retirement" by checking in with Captain Maggie everyday. The family has another generation of ferrymen waiting to come of age. (Trimble photograph.)

The Golden Gate Bridge, Highway and Transportation District's M. V. Sonoma, one of the district's three original boats, is en route to San Francisco from Sausalito on July 16, 2006, using the same lane as the steamers once did for the Northwestern Pacific. (Trimble photograph.)

Larkspur Landing is a transit complex consisting of ferry docks, bus stops for district buses, a large capacity parking lot for automobiles, pedestrian paths, paved roadways, and cycling lanes to the town of Larkspur in Marin County. M. V. *Del Norte* (left) and M. V. *Sonoma* (right) are docked side by side. (Trimble photograph.)

M. V. *Mendocino* is the newest of the five ferries of the Golden Gate Bridge, Highway and Transportation District, having been built in 2001. The high-speed catamaran operates regularly between Larkspur Landing and San Francisco. (Trimble photograph.)

The Blue and Gold Fleet also operates ferries to Tiburon, and here, on August 13, 2006, the *Bay Monarch* discharged patrons at the dock in Tiburon at about the same place the ferries of the SF&NP would off-load people. Today there is little trace of the SF&NP. (Trimble photograph.)

Two San Francisco landmarks, Pier No. 39 at left and Coit Tower at right, form the background for a lineup of afternoon ferries to Alameda County. Pictured from left to right are *Oski*, *Old Blue* (partially hidden), *Golden Bear* of the Blue and Gold Fleet, and *Encinal* of Alameda Ferry. (Trimble photograph.)

The Blue and Gold Fleet's *Old Blue* departs from Pier No. 41 in San Francisco, bound for the East Bay with another load of commuters. Maneuvering through tight spaces was not the forte of paddle wheelers, something the modern boats do with ease. (Trimble photograph.)

Owned by the City of Alameda, across the estuary from Oakland, the M. V. *Peralta* arrives at Oakland's Jack London Square at the foot of Clay Street. Container ships, small craft, ferries, and the former presidential yacht *Potomac* (out of view) make the Port of Oakland a busy place. (Trimble photograph.)

On September 6, 2006, the Vallejo BayLink catamaran ferry *Mare Island* docks at the Ferry Building, boarding passengers for another trip to Vallejo. Owned by the city of Vallejo, BayLink ferries are manned by Blue and Gold Fleet crews. At right is the GGBH&TD's *San Francisco*, in from Sausalito. (Trimble photograph.)

The high-speed catamaran ferry *Solano* of Vallejo BayLink Ferry arrives at San Francisco's Ferry Building at 6:30 p.m. on September 1, 2006, right on time. BayLink ferries are owned by the City of Vallejo but manned by Blue and Gold Fleet crews. (Trimble photograph.)

About 7:23 p.m. on September 6, 2006, a fog settles over San Francisco Bay as the Alameda-Oakland Ferry *Encinal* heads into San Francisco from Jack London Square in Oakland and Alameda, trailed by the Harbor Bay Ferry *Bay Breeze*, in from Alameda's Bay Farm Island. (Trimble photograph.)

The Harbor Bay Ferry catamaran *Bay Breeze* arrives at the Ferry Building from Alameda's Bay Farm Island at 7:30 p.m. In the background is the Bay Bridge, built to replace the ferries. Ironically, bridge and freeway traffic congestion has diverted people back to ferryboats. (Trimble photograph.)

GLOSSARY

A-FRAME: An A-shaped framework supporting the walking beam.

AFT: Pertaining to the rear end, toward the rear.

AMIDSHIPS: Center of a vessel, between fore and aft.

APRON: A runway for boarding a ferry from a dock, resting on the deck to adjust to the tides.

BEAM: The extreme width of a vessel's hull.

BELOWDECKS: decks below the cabin deck.

BOW, STEM: Front end of a ship or boat.

CABIN DECK, SALOON DECK: The first deck above the maindeck, usually for passengers.

COMPOUND ENGINE: A steam engine in which the steam is used twice, first for a high pressure cylinder and again in a low pressure cylinder.

DOUBLE-ENDER: A ferry in which either end can be the bow and can travel equally in either direction.

EYE SPLICE: A rope or hawser with a loop spliced onto the end.

FIDLEY, FIDDLEY: Section in the center of a vessel devoted to the engine and connecting apparatus to the engine.

FORE, FORWARD: Pertaining to the front end, toward the front.

GUYS: Ropes or wires used to give support to parts of a vessel.

HAWSER: Large diameter ropes used for mooring lines.

HOGPOST: A tall mast in the center of a ferry or riverboat to secure guys; used for towing lines on a riverboat.

HULL: The main part of a vessel; the part that floats in the water.

HURRICANE DECK: The top deck of a ferry or riverboat, usually closed to the public.

JACKSTAFF: A flagpole on a vessel.

MAINDECK: The first deck above the waterline.

PILOTHOUSE, WHEELHOUSE: Steering cabin on a vessel; also houses whistle and bell controls and communications apparatus to the engine room.

PORT, PORTSIDE: Left side of a vessel when facing forward.

RIVERBOAT: A vessel designed for travel on inland waters, usually single ended.

SHIP'S TELEGRAPH: A mechanical device for the captain or pilot to signal to the engine room to shut the engines off or on, the direction of travel and speed.

SIDEWHEELER: Having paddle wheels on the sides of a hull.

SINGLE ENDER: A ferry having both a bow and a stern.

SISTER SHIPS: Two or more vessels constructed from the same blueprints.

SLIP: Dock for a ferryboat.

SPONSON: Overhang of a ferry or riverboat beyond the side of the hull.

STACK, FUNNEL: Large cylinder for drawing up the engine's exhaust; chimney.

STARBOARD: The right side of a ship or boat when facing forward.

STERN: Back end of a ship or boat.

STERNWHEELER: Vessel with a paddle wheel at the stern.

TEXAS: The deck above the cabin deck.

TILLER: A bar used to steer a vessel in lieu of a wheel.

WAKE, WASH: Water pattern left from a moving vessel.

WALKING BEAM: A diamond shaped framework attached to a piston on one end and a crankshaft on the other end connected to an eccentric shaft transferring energy from the engine to the paddle wheels.

WATER LINE: A vessel's line of flotation.

Visit us at
arcadiapublishing.com

www.ingramcontent.com/pod-product-compliance
Lightning Source LLC
Chambersburg PA
CBHW080630110426
42813CB00006B/1647